The Secret C

Straight talking about cancer

Julie A. Stokes OBE

Illustrated by Peter Bailey

Foreword by HRH The Prince of Wales

Winston's Wish

in association with Macmillan Cancer Support

For Debra whose sparkle inspired this book.

JS

*The author would like to thank the following children
for all their invaluable help:*
*Abigail, Ali, Ben, Charlotte, Gary, James, John, Kate,
Katie, Mark, Michelle and Paula.*

ST. JAMES'S PALACE

The Secret C is a children's book, but it also gives a clear message to adults. Children are never too young to be included when an illness like cancer affects someone who is important to them.

We all like to be given, by people we trust, information we can easily understand. It helps us if we can ask questions freely, knowing that someone will listen for the real meaning behind our words and answer truthfully. Cancer is a hugely complex condition, involving a vast number of very different types of disease, with many different kinds of treatment and very different success rates. Somehow, this ingenious book has managed to distil that complexity into the issues that are key for children.

I am sure that this text will help children ask the questions that they need to ask and will help adults to answer them. These questions may come at desperately inconvenient and inappropriate times, so we need to be prepared. However difficult we find this, as parents, teachers, nurses or carers, we watch with pride as we see our children cope with events that remind us all of the fragility and beauty of life.

The trouble with cancer is that doctors
don't yet understand why people get it.
Why do people talk about it in whispers?
Where does it come from?
Why is it hard to make the person better?
Will I get cancer too?

When someone in your family has cancer, everything changes.

Perhaps you feel angry.

Or sad.

Or fed up.

Or scared.

Or maybe all of these.

Perhaps you think,

It's not fair!

Maybe you feel guilty as if somehow it's all your fault. It isn't. Nobody gets cancer because of something you did or didn't do.

And you can't catch cancer either.

Most children want to know when someone they care about has cancer.

This is what happens.
Everyone's body is made up of millions of
tiny cells, so small you need a microscope
to see them.
When we're healthy, these cells work hard.
Then they wear out and are replaced with
new ones.

But sometimes, something goes wrong.
Instead of behaving themselves, some cells
grow too quickly and they start to crowd
out the good cells.
Often they stick together and form a lump,
a tumour. There are lots of different cancers.
Some are serious and some are not.
Grown-ups can get cancer and sometimes
even children get cancer.

My Daddy was really sick. I know
how it happened. How the tumour got
there. The white cells played a
trick on it. That's what happened.

Cancer is a
very serious
disease.

If someone has cancer, they have to go
to hospital. The doctors will try different
ways to make them better.
Sometimes the person will have an
operation to cut out the tumour.

11

They may have radiotherapy – special
rays are aimed at the cancer cells.
Radiotherapy can make a person feel very
tired. Too tired to play.

They may have chemotherapy as well –
special medicine to zap the cancer cells.
Chemotherapy can make a person feel sick
too and sometimes their hair falls out.
It doesn't hurt and it grows back but it
can be hard to get used to.

When Dad was very ill, he used to be sick a lot.
Once I was eating my tea when he was sick.

The doctors try to make Mum better
by giving her tablets.

Sometimes, when someone is having treatment, it's difficult to know what to do. You can help by fetching them drinks or snacks, reading to them, drawing them pictures, talking to them and telling them jokes.

Or if they feel very unwell, you can
just sit quietly by their bed and keep
them company.
You can spend time with them at home,
or at the hospital, or on the telephone.
Just be yourself!

Mum looked really different.
She seemed to have changed
completely.
She's changed
a lot.

At first I felt like I was in the way and
Mum thought I was a pain, but she didn't.

It can be really annoying when someone is too tired to play with you.

And it can be hard to have a good time when someone is in pain.

But remember, it is ok to enjoy yourself even if someone in your family is ill.

It's not easy having a brother with cancer.
We like to fight but now I'm worried
I might hurt him and Mum will get cross
with me. I just want to do what's best —
I wish I knew what that was...

The treatment for cancer can take a long time. It's not easy to have a sick person in the family. People at school may not understand about cancer. They may even tease you. If this happens, it's important to ask your teacher to explain to them what cancer means. Don't feel you have to keep everything to yourself.

You should talk to your best friend.
Other people sometimes walk out on you
Perhaps they don't know what to say.

You might have a lot of questions. Is there someone you can talk to, someone you trust, who will tell you the truth about what's happening?

When someone is ill, there are lots
of telephone calls, visitors, hospital visits
and conversations behind closed doors.
It's easy to feel left out. And it's easy to
get very angry and say hurtful things that
you wish you hadn't said.
It's hard for the person who is sick and
it's hard for you too!

I used to think if I wasn't naughty, it would make the cancer go away. Being good is hard, but I try my best.

When Mum was first ill, I was really angry with her.

Sometimes the cancer comes back. It's very upsetting when this happens. But there are all sorts of medicines and treatments to try to make people with cancer better.
And lots of people do get better and are never ill with cancer again.

Sometimes, even though everyone has done their best, the cancer doesn't go away forever. If this happens, the person may not get better. This is a difficult thing to think about. "When mum first told me that dad's treatment might not cure the cancer forever, I was angry. Later I gave her a hug and we cried together. It was hard to hear but I'm pleased she could trust me."

This is BIG stuff to deal with. The grown-ups around you will realise that you have questions and need to be kept informed. Speak to the nurse or maybe mention it to a teacher you trust at school?

I never cried at school.
If I cried it would be at night.
Miss Maloney seemed to understand and asked
me quietly how things were at home...

When someone is very unwell, they may want to think about the good times.
You could make a fantastic book together, with photographs and drawings of all the things you want to remember

This would be nice for you to keep.

When someone in the family is ill, there are still things to be done, like going to school, and eating your meals and cleaning your teeth. And it's really important that you still find time for fun!

31

All over the world scientists and doctors
are trying to solve the secret of cancer.
They have already found cures for some
cancers but there's still a lot of work that
needs to be done.
We all hope that one day everybody can
be cured of cancer. When this happens
we will have the *biggest* party ever.
After all ...